PLANNING YOUR DREAMS

Dreams Are The Plans Of Our Future

ISBN: 978-0-9715510-3-9

Publisher: Arlette Thomas-Fletcher

Shining Bright Productions LLC

Dream Plan Series

For more information or to contact the author send inquiries to:Arlettethomasfletcher.com

https://www.arlettethomasfletcher.com/projects-2

To Dream

By Arlette Thomas-Fletcher

A **dream** is but a whisper in the recesses of our **minds**.

They can be **snatched** over the course of time.

If we wait too long, they **fade** away with the tide.

As the water returns to the ocean so can our dreams **drift** away.

But we must not let this happen because our dreams are **tiny diamonds shining bright** like stars in the night sky, drawing us to look up at the beauty of the wonders they bring.

So, do not **fail the dream** by having no plan.

For every dream needs a guide to find its way to the **magical place** in your heart.

So be true and **faithful** to yourself and achieve your goals and make sure your dream has a dream plan.

Dreams are not to be **forgotten** or passed off as just mere chances.

But dreams are met to be **challenges** to something greater than ourselves.

If we must dream, let us **dream high** and reach for the sky never letting gravity pull us to the ground.

So, dream we must, but **work hard** too, so that we can make all our dreams come true.

DEDICATION

This book is dedicated to my mother, Inez Rosebud Thomas, who taught me to dream and that there was nothing in the world I could not achieve. She inspired all her children to work hard to achieve their goals and to be the best they could be in life. She believed that dreams were important and that you should not let anything hold you back from going to college or getting training to have the desired career.

She was a loving and giving human being who always inspired her children, grandchildren, and anyone she could motivate to achieve their best in life.

To Kenneth, my husband, who has always supported me in achieving my dreams and goals for over twenty years; Charles and Joel, my sons, who grew up dreaming and are now living the life they dreamed of because of their hard work and faith in God.

ACKNOWLEDGMENT

Everything I write comes from the inspiration that the Lord has given me. I am truly excited about the opportunity to write this book. I want to honor the Lord Jesus Christ, my Savior, for giving me something I can share with young people so they can learn how to plan their dreams. God gave all of us dreams, and He wants us to fulfill our purpose.

I am humbled to see my own dreams come true by completing this book as an author. This would not be possible without the guidance of my Lord and Savior, Jesus Christ, who is the author and finisher of my faith. So, I would like to honor and thank God, from whom all blessings flow.

Table of Contents

FOREWORD

My purpose for writing the Planning Your Dreams Workbook and Self-Help book is to help teenagers begin to think about their future. Often, children don't have any idea what they want to do with their lives. Having a book to look at regarding their dreams and the possibilities of what they can do with their lives is a really good tool for them to have.

My own children needed guidance to understand how to plan for their futures. One of the greatest ways for children to explore the choices they have for a career in life is to dream, ponder the unknown, and look at what others are doing.

That is what this book is about: taking the stress off a child's mind and helping them to realize that they can be anything they want to be with a plan. This book has areas where a teen can fill in and work through what they are thinking and map out how they want to become a doctor, lawyer, teacher, fireman, nurse, or whatever they desire to become. It takes the pressure off the parents who are always trying to get their children to think about what they want to do with their lives when they graduate from high school.

The teen can sit down and just dream about all the possibilities of what they might want to do because there are examples in this book of different occupations that other people are working in successfully. It is a dream and a plan of what the world has to offer as a career and how you can plan for it just by sitting down and working through the workbook.

WHAT IS A DREAM?

A dream is a picture of what we want to achieve with our lives, which we create in our minds over time, from childhood. A dream is a vision of who and what we want to be in the future. It starts from the mind and the heart. You cannot achieve what your mind and heart have not conceived without guidance. Dreams are woven together from childhood.

A dream is more than what you are good at. Many people think that dreams are connected to what you are good at, and that is what you should do with your life. But just because you are good at raking the yard doesn't mean you should be a landscaper. Just because you are good at fixing cars doesn't mean you should be a mechanic. Sometimes people are good at things they don't like or want to do with their lives.

It is true that childhood dreams are interwoven with fantasies, which are influenced by the movies and books you read. However, as people grow, they can differentiate fantasies from their dreams. They may drop the fantasies as they face the reality of life, but the dreams live in them.

Children must be encouraged to express their dreams so that their parents or guardians can help them structure their dreams appropriately. A child may say, "I dream of being a supermodel one day!" But this may never happen to that child for reasons that no one even understands. This is why some dreams can be considered unrealistic. Parents should encourage children to dream, but dreams must be tempered with reality.

Many people grow up not living the dreams they have woven into their minds due to many factors. This is the reason many people are frustrated with their lives.

If you took a survey of most people in the work world today, you would find that most people don't like what they are doing.

If you love to run, then run and enjoy what running brings to your life. A person who loves running should not be confined to sitting in a chair daily looking at a computer screen. If you love the outdoors, working in an office is not for you. You want to be able to travel and move around.

Doing something you don't like can lead to disappointment and frustration. It can also lead to stress and health problems. Depression in adults may be linked to unfulfilled dreams or doing something without inner motivation.

This is why Dream Planning is essential. Dream planning is about doing what stimulates your inner being, your soul! A great person once said, "**If you do what you** love to do then you will never work a day in your life."

When should a person start a dream plan?

A dream plan should be started when you are at least twelve or fifteen years old at the latest. Some of us started dreaming of what we wanted to do when we were five or so and stuck with that our whole lives. However, most people start out saying, "I want to be a doctor, lawyer, model, or something else," and then, as they get older, their plans change.

Think About It

It is better to have a plan on how you will work out your dreams and start taking deliberate and calculated steps towards it. Don't wait until you are old. You will avoid making many mistakes and wasting time if you plan your dream now while you are young.

DREAM INDICATORS

The first step to starting your dream plan is looking at the things you enjoy doing or do with passion without anyone pushing you to do them. Dreams and passion are closely related.

What is your passion? What are the things that make your soul light up? Your dreams! You just have to take the time to imagine them. Think about the things that bring you joy. Ponder on them because those are the things that help us form our dreams. For example:

I like to play video games all the time.

Maybe you could be a person that creates video games, but you must remember that you cannot create video games while you play video games all day. If you want it as a career, then you have to take the time to learn the process of creating these games.

You could also be a person that creates artificial intelligence that is used in military battle.

I like making sure things are secured.

Maybe you can do cyber security.

Maybe you would be good at Homeland Security.

I love to eat good food and how I feel when I am in a restaurant environment.

Maybe you want to be a chef or a cook.

I like helping people when they are in trouble.

Maybe you would be good at being a social worker.

A fireman

A nurse

I like being outdoors around animals. I love to see the earth and its beauty.

Maybe you would be good at being a forest ranger.

An environmentalist

I love to look at the stars.

Maybe you would be a good astronomer.

These are examples of careers you can pursue in the future if you enjoy these activities. Let's start by identifying your dream indicator.

The dream indicator has been seen in many famous people, like Martin Luther King, Nelson Mandela, Lebron James, Roger Federer, Serena Williams, and many others. How do we know this? We know this because Martin Luther King's dream changed the world for civil rights.

Nelson Mandela changed South Africa's way of Apartheid. These are just some examples of dreams changing a person and the life of a society.

Think About It.

Look at the things you do effortlessly and with enthusiasm because they may be pointers or indicators of what you should do with your life.

WHAT IS A DREAM PLAN?

A plan is a detailed proposal for achieving a goal. It involves stating the steps and methods required to achieve a goal. It also includes setting time aside and allocating resources to achieve a dream.

A dream plan is, therefore, all the goals and means you intend to achieve your dreams. A dream plan involves setting goals, setting time, and allocating resources to achieve your dreams. A dream is something you want to do that may be larger than life. For dreams to come true, goals must be set to accomplish the dreams. Also, when reaching for the dream, one must be honest with him/herself.

What does this mean?

All dreams don't always work out for everyone. Goals are important for achieving the aspirations that we have in our dreams.

Plans must be made to achieve the goals that will get us to our dreams. If we try to achieve our dreams and things are not moving in the direction of our dreams, we have to re-evaluate and determine if this is a possible and viable objective. We should always try for our dreams because it is important to know we tried, even if it does not materialize into what we want.

It is harder to accept that something didn't work out when you have never tried to see if it would work. Being honest with yourself is very important when making plans to achieve the goals that make your dreams come true.

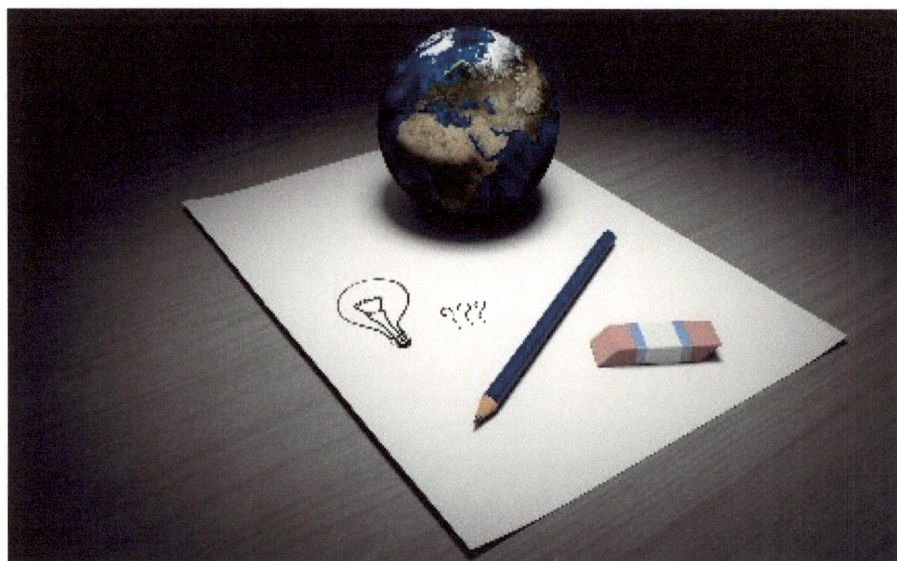

DREAM PLAN

Jot down some of your goals.

Short Term Goals

_____

_____

_____

_____

_____

_____

_____

_____

_____

_____

_____

_____

_____

Long Term Goals

_____

_____

_____

_____

_____

_____

_____

_____

_____

_____

_____

_____

_____

_____

Think About It.

If you fail to plan, you are planning to fail. Planning should precede all achievement. You cannot achieve your dreams by accident, you have to plan for it.

DREAM BIG - WORK HARD

WORKING OUT YOUR DREAM IN REALITY

As was stated before, not all dreams are realistic. Childhood dreams are laced with fantasies. As you grow, you will begin to differentiate between dreams and fantasies. The reality of life may adjust or sharpen the expression of the dream. You must know how to analyze your situation and make decisions that will suit your dreams without affecting your responsibilities. For example:

Scenario:

You want to be a famous singer? You work hard and sing publicly in many places.

Everyone loves your singing, but you have children to feed and bills to pay. How can you pursue your dreams while also fulfilling your responsibilities?

Decision:

Work your job, sing, and perform as much as possible at different events. Take advantage of opportunities as much as your schedule permits. Don't forget your responsibilities. Set goals to move your dream forward, never forgetting your responsibilities. If you have an opportunity to go on "The Voice," go! Save your money as much as you can and work hard to achieve your goals as you try out for new opportunities. So, you must know how to pursue your dreams without being reckless or irresponsible. It may require you to work extra hours to raise enough money to fulfill your dream. That is how to work out your dreams with reality.

What's your Life Scenario?

Life Scenario:

_____

_____

_____

_____

_____

_____

_____

_____

_____

_____

_____

_____

_____

Options:

_____

_____

_____

_____

_____

_____

_____

_____

_____

_____

_____

_____

_____

_____

Decision:

_____

_____

_____

_____

_____

_____

_____

_____

_____

_____

_____

_____

_____

_____

Think About It:

Pursuing your dreams may require that you go the extra mile because you must consider other components to complete your dream goals.

ANALYZE YOUR DREAM

Number your list in order of priority, 1-10, ten being the highest number.

LIST THE THINGS YOU LOVE TO DO

_____

_____

_____

_____

_____

_____

_____

_____

_____

_____

_____

_____

LIST YOUR STRENGTHS

LIST YOUR WEAKNESS

_____

_____

_____

_____

_____

_____

_____

_____

_____

_____

_____

_____

_____

THINGS YOU LOVE TO DO:

_____

_____

_____

_____

_____

_____

_____

_____

_____

_____

_____

_____

_____

_____

STRENGTHS

_____

_____

_____

_____

_____

_____

_____

_____

_____

_____

_____

_____

_____

_____

WEAKNESS

_____

_____

_____

_____

_____

_____

_____

_____

_____

_____

_____

_____

_____

_____

NURTURING YOUR DREAM

DREAM PLAN

1. Take the things you love to do and determine the highest on your list based on the numbers 1-10. These are things that you would want to do every day as a job.

2. Look at the things you are good at and see if anything coincides with what you love to do.

3. Don't worry if you are not good at what you love to do.

4. Remember, you can get training and education to learn how to do what you love to do. (Make sure it's realistic but don't limit yourself too much.)

5. Start looking at the goals you need to set to achieve what you love to do.

6. Begin to research the kinds of education and training that will be required to achieve what you are aspiring to be.

7. Align yourself with a mentor in the field that you are thinking of pursuing.

8. Ask the mentor questions regarding how they achieved their goals.

9. Remember that failure is a lesson in learning and does not mean that you should quit.

10. Analyze where you are at each step of your journey to reach the goals of your dream.

11. Surround yourself with people who are dream achievers, especially in the things you want to achieve.

12. Don't let negative voices interfere with your goals.

13. Remember to be rational and not set unrealistic goals or even dreams that may disappoint you because they are impossible to reach.

14. Stay focused and keep working on the plan even if it seems hard to do. Remember, this is what you want to do with your life, but be honest with yourself. If you have done all the research to assure you that it will work for you, then you will already know in your heart if it is realistic for you.

15. Remember, it all has to be done in stages, so start with your dreams and goals. Make sure you incorporate what you love to do. Then make sure you map out how you want to do it. Finally, implementation of your dream plan is a process of combining everything you have worked on and putting it into action in your life every day.

Think About It:

For your dream to come together, you must utilize all the components you placed on your list to have a great dream plan.

DEVELOPING YOUR DREAM PLAN

LIST THINGS YOU LOVE TO DO

Make a list of things that you value. Take time to think about it and mow it over. Relax and just take your time and make the list as long as you like.

Nothing is silly; you are just looking at things you like to do. Don't worry about any order now; you are just brainstorming to determine how you feel about things. Sometimes, if you get stuck, don't worry about it; just take a drive, or go for a walk. This will stimulate you to think about your future plans.

USE YOUR IMAGINATION

Start to look at the things you have put on your list that you adore. Begin thinking of yourself doing those things for the rest of your life. Start to daydream about how it would feel to do what you are fond of doing. The ones that stand out the most will be the most important. Begin to research the types of jobs associated with what you are attracted to doing and would delight in doing every day of your life.

LOOK AT YOUR STRENGTHS

Begin to list all the things you think you are good at doing. Don't hold back because this is just to get your juices going. Remember, this list could be very long. Don't worry if it's short either. You can list anything on it, from being

48

good at cooking to running a race. This is not a stressful exercise, so don't try and think too much. Just let all your ideas flow. You can ask friends, parents, etc., about things you are good at if you need someone to verify these things with you. Remember, you are an awesome individual who wants to feel good about what you do every day, and you can.

Admit you have Weaknesses

You may not be an artistic person who can draw, paint, dance, or even sing. Talent is not just in the ability to sing or dance. Talent can also be in the ability to build and construct something special. Talent can also be in doing a great report or coming up with an awesome process!

It doesn't matter if you are great at sports or any kind of athletics. What matters is that you have your own genuine skill that comes from the uniqueness of your makeup.

DREAM PLAN

Now that you have looked at the things you appreciate doing and everything you aspire to accomplish, it is time to move to your next step. Make a list of your strengths and your weaknesses. Now, it is time to put your dream plan together.

Let's start with the things you are good at achieving. Maybe you are good at cooking. But you don't really like to cook. But your strengths are in creating recipes and writing. Possibly you like teaching others how to make new dishes, but you don't want to be the one to make them. So maybe you are a cookbook author. Possibly, you create recipes that people or chefs use to make special dishes.

Maybe you enjoy exercise classes and just can't wait to get there every week. You also like dancing, moving, riding bikes, and being active. What if your mother is an accountant and your father is a computer analyst? These are good jobs that pay well. But the job your parents tell you to do requires you to sit behind a desk every day, just like they are doing.

You don't have to do what your parents did. You can be a fitness coach, or you could open your own fitness center. To do things like this, you often have to start out in an entry-level position and work your way up. But the key here is to do what you love, not just a job.

It is so easy to just go to school and focus on a major, but dreams are important, and we need to give space to our dreams. Some of the greatest people in history achieved their dreams through hard work and perseverance. Steve Jobs and Bill Gates started their businesses out of their parents' garages while they were teenagers.

"Madison Robinson, a 15-year-old created Flip flops, originally only selling flip-flops with teen centric designs. She soon branched out to include other apparel and even a complementary app earning $1 million in sales before she could drive. She epitomizes entrepreneur."

Source: smallbusinessyahoo.com

"Elise MacMillan teamed up with her grandmother to make candy ever since she was a toddler. At 11, she worked with her brother in a commercial chocolatier and founded the Chocolate Farm. She earned top spots on the lists by Ernst & Young and several other accolades."

Source: https://trendcatchers.co.uk

"Julianne Goldmark and Emily Matson created hair ties, getting inspiration in the eighth grade when they envied celebrity high-end ties but couldn't afford them. By their senior year of high school, the friends had cashed in on a connection one of their moms had to Jennifer Aniston, and they now make about $10 million per year."

Source: http://inspirationsmv.com/

"Connor Zwick started toying with JavaScript in middle school, and by 19 was making some of the most in-demand tutorials in the industry. The builder of the Flashcards+ app, Zwick eventually dropped out of Harvard to study under PayPal's founder."

Source: https://www.inc.com

Scott and Stacy Ferreira is a brother-sister duo that launched MySocialCloud.com when Scott was in college and Stacy was still in high school. However, their entrepreneurial spirit was sparked as young children watching their father work at IBM and Goggle."

Source: https://www.businessinsider.com

"Abbey Fleck was the inventor of Makin' Bacon and designed the first microwave bacon cooking technology when she was just 8. A favorite on the infomercial circuit, she's been featured on numerous talk shows."

Source: Inc.com.John boitnott

Think About It

You are not too young to dream or pursue your dreams.

CREATE YOUR DREAMS

Step I: Goals and Dreams

Step II: What I love to do

_____

_____

_____

_____

_____

_____

_____

_____

_____

_____

_____

_____

Step III: How I plan to do it

_____

_____

_____

_____

_____

_____

_____

_____

_____

_____

_____

_____

Step IV: Implementation: Putting it into action

_____

_____

_____

_____

_____

_____

_____

_____

_____

_____

_____

_____

_____

_____

Notes

Notes

_____

_____

_____

_____

_____

_____

_____

_____

_____

_____

_____

_____

_____

_____

Notes

_____

_____

_____

_____

_____

_____

_____

_____

_____

_____

_____

_____

_____

_____

Notes

_____

_____

_____

_____

_____

_____

_____

_____

_____

_____

_____

_____

_____

_____

Notes

_____

_____

_____

_____

_____

_____

_____

_____

_____

_____

_____

_____

_____

Notes

Notes

_____

_____

_____

_____

_____

_____

_____

_____

_____

_____

_____

_____

_____

Notes

_____

_____

_____

_____

_____

_____

_____

_____

_____

_____

_____

_____

_____

_____

Notes

_____

_____

_____

_____

_____

_____

_____

_____

_____

_____

_____

_____

_____

Start Your Dream Journal

Use these action words in this Dream Journal to start to write about all aspects of your dreams.

_____

_____

_____

_____

_____

_____

_____

_____

_____

_____

_____

_____

_____

Dreaming

_____

_____

_____

_____

_____

_____

_____

_____

_____

_____

_____

_____

_____

Imagining

_____

_____

_____

_____

_____

_____

_____

_____

_____

_____

_____

_____

_____

_____

Pondering

_____

_____

_____

_____

_____

_____

_____

_____

_____

_____

_____

_____

Planning

_____

_____

_____

_____

_____

_____

_____

_____

_____

_____

_____

_____

_____

_____

Building

_____

_____

_____

_____

_____

_____

_____

_____

_____

_____

_____

_____

_____

Constructing

_____

_____

_____

_____

_____

_____

_____

_____

_____

_____

_____

_____

_____

_____

_____

Believing

_____

_____

_____

_____

_____

_____

_____

_____

_____

_____

_____

_____

_____

_____

Trusting

_____

_____

_____

_____

_____

_____

_____

_____

_____

_____

_____

_____

_____

Enjoying

Thinking

_____

_____

_____

_____

_____

_____

_____

_____

_____

_____

_____

_____

_____

Projecting

Envisioning

_____

_____

_____

_____

_____

_____

_____

_____

_____

_____

_____

_____

_____

Learning

Growing

_____

_____

_____

_____

_____

_____

_____

_____

_____

_____

_____

_____

_____

Visualizing

Developing

_____

_____

_____

_____

_____

_____

_____

_____

_____

_____

_____

_____

_____

_____

Formulating

Idea | To do | Doing | Done

Scheduling

_____

_____

_____

_____

_____

_____

_____

_____

_____

_____

_____

_____

_____

Arranging

Preparing

_____

_____

_____

_____

_____

_____

_____

_____

_____

_____

_____

_____

_____

_____

Partnering

_____

_____

_____

_____

_____

_____

_____

_____

_____

_____

_____

_____

_____

Maturing

_____

_____

_____

_____

_____

_____

_____

_____

_____

_____

_____

_____

_____

_____

Climbing

_____

_____

_____

_____

_____

_____

_____

_____

_____

_____

_____

_____

_____

Breaking Through

_____

_____

_____

_____

_____

_____

_____

_____

_____

_____

_____

_____

Creating

_____

_____

_____

_____

_____

_____

_____

_____

_____

_____

_____

_____

_____

Considering

_____

_____

_____

_____

_____

_____

_____

_____

_____

_____

_____

_____

_____

_____

Rising

_____

_____

_____

_____

_____

_____

_____

_____

_____

_____

_____

_____

_____

_____

Plotting

_____

_____

_____

_____

_____

_____

_____

_____

_____

_____

_____

_____

_____

_____

Planting

_____

_____

_____

_____

_____

_____

_____

_____

_____

_____

_____

_____

_____

_____

Harvesting

_____

_____

_____

_____

_____

_____

_____

_____

_____

_____

_____

_____

_____

_____

Working

Activating

Celebrating

_____

_____

_____

_____

_____

_____

_____

_____

_____

_____

_____

_____

_____

_____

_____

Other Books By The Author

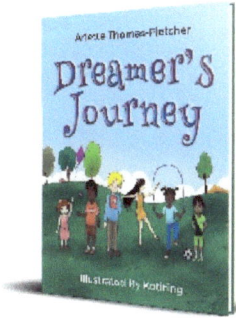

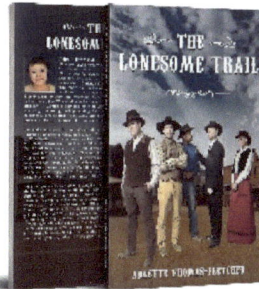

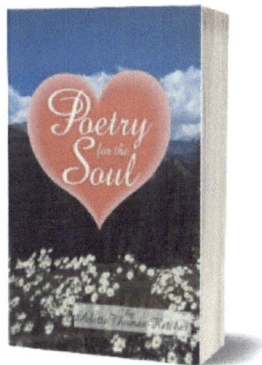

https://www.arlettethomasfletcher.com/projects-2

PLANNING YOUR DREAMS

Arlette Thomas-Fletcher is a dreamer! She truly wants to manifest God's Dream inside of her spirit through her writing, filmmaking and music. While working a full-time job she has pursued her dream of being a writer, filmmaker, playwright, and vocalist. She was the president of Women and Film and Video of Maryland for ten years. She worked very hard to achieve her dreams. Over the years she worked on numerous projects.

She was able to write, direct and produce her first Christian western feature film called "The Lonesome Trail" which has won 18 awards and 2 nominations. "The Lonesome Trail Christian western film is now available on Video on Demand (VOD) on Amazon Prime, YouTube, Vimeo, Comcast, Verizon Fios, Dish TV and many other VOD platforms. Her Song "You're Not Alone" was the selection of the International Christian Music Awards. Her other song "Jesus You Are the One I Depend On" and "If My People" have been nominated for Best Performance Artist at the International Christian Film and Music Festival. She is an award-winning screenwriter for screenplays such as "Assault in Brooklyn", "The Lonesome Trail", and The Legend of Carter Dodson.

Since she was a child, she has dreamed of writing stories plays, films, books and songs that would touch the hearts of people. In her life she has been able to accomplish her dreams by writing books, stage-plays, screenplays, song lyrics and articles. She is a minister of the Gospel of the Lord Jesus Christ and is humbled to be a vessel of God. Her work has been inspired by God and she is humbled to have this talent to share with others. She believes that everyday is a new opportunity to reach your goals. She is a wife and mother of two wonderful sons. She truly feels honored to have them in her life and feels that they have been a true inspiration to her work by the support and love they give her every day. She has devoted her life to God for many years. She genuinely enjoys honoring the Lord Jesus Christ through the ministry in all forms of media.

This ministry is shown by her many works to glorify God in her writings, sermons, songs, and other works. It is truly an honor for her to pour out from her spirit what God has ministered to her to the people of God and the world at large. Arlette holds a master's degree in Business from one of the most prestigious institutions in the country Johns Hopkins University.

She is also an Elder at Words of Wisdom Fellowship Church. She has frequently been engaged as a lecturer, orator and vocalist at colleges and universities and faith organizations. She is also an author of the book Poetry for The Soul inspirational poetry book, The Lonesome Trail Christian western book, and Dreamer's Journey children's book. She has written children's books that are in development. Arlette resides in Maryland with her husband and two sons.

www.ingramcontent.com/pod-product-compliance
Lightning Source LLC
Chambersburg PA
CBHW041103110426
42740CB00043B/138